KIDSTUFF

ITV BOOKS

Published by

Independent Television Books Ltd
247 Tottenham Court Road
London W1P 0AU

In association with Michael Joseph Ltd

First published 1980
© Roger Goffe, 1980

ISBN 0 900727 78 0

Conditions of Sale

Printed by Dai Nippon Printing (Europa) GMBH

KIDSTUFF

BY ROGER

ITV BOOKS

in association with

MICHAEL JOSEPH

Sorry that Im so late for school miss but Im a very slow sleeper!

in "Bob a Job" week we all collect old newspapers and dirty books!

My baby brother was born Just after Mum finished being pregnant!

I would have won the running race but I heard mum calling my name, so I stopped to see what she wanted!

yesterday you said that three fours make twelve, and now you say two sixes make twelve! what's the matter, cant you make up your mind?

Dad said that at least my rotten marks at school prove that I havent been cheating!

water is sterile after its boiled and allowed to dry!

My rabbit died on Sunday so we had carrots for lunch!

Sorry I cant tell you my secret wish for my birthday! I dont think I'll get one anyway, because we dont even have a stable!

My thankyou letter to my friend Lucy is badly written but she wont mind 'cos she cant ~~see~~ read any way!

Worms cant fly,
so why do the
birds wait up
in the trees?

Mum! please
come and
switch off
this dark.
I'm frightened!

At the zoo
I saw a big
tortoise flying
underwater!

Our cat Kissed the Budgie and it disappeared!

Some people have longer arms than others, it all depends where your sleeves end!

I am good but I have wild hands that take things!

Dad has fur under his arms I think his stuffing is coming out!

Is "willing" Gods second name?

When the trees wave to each other it always starts to get windy!

Teacher said they ring birds to find out where they fly to. I didnt even know they had phones!

Someones Coming! I can hear their footprints on the stairs!

Mum, why do you Keep standing on the scales if they always make you angry?

Mum and Dad spent ages teaching me to walk and talk, and now I go to school the teacher always tells me to shut up and sit down!

We all went to the park except Mum, she stayed home because she said she just couldn't leave the builder alone!

Please take a
Pretty photo
of me as
I was ugly
on the one
you took last
time!

Robbers are
People who
borrow things
without asking
and never
bring them back!

My brother
can wink! But
only when I
stick a finger
in his eye!

Every Monday council men with a big lorry come and steal everything from our dustbin!

Mum, why did you say you'll go crazy if I ask any more questions?

My Mum has a prayer for me she says "Thank God!" when I go to bed!

When dad has been to the pub I can smell his words!

My Mum was Dads girlfriend, but things are different now they're married!

I know we get milk from cows, but what animal do we get our soup from?

Also, if you know it was me who let Dads ferrets out, please tell me before you tell my Dad. Thankyou God!

I feel exhausted! when I woke up this morning both my eyes were still open!

Have a chocolate. The ones with teeth marks are caramel!

Do you still get into trouble if you rob a bank by accident?

When I was first born, my dad had a celebration, but Mum had an early night instead!

Our vicar must be very poor! His church windows dont even have curtains!

Dont talk to someone you dont know, They might be a stranger!

Walking would be very difficult if our legs werent split down the middle!

My friend lives on the third shelf of a large block of flats.

Mum, why aren't pigs striped the same as bacon?

Robbers are people who run into banks with pistol guns and shout "stick it up!"

I dont understand food, I've been eating it for years and I'm not full yet!

On the farm, they live in sties, grunt, and eat swill! No wonder they're called Pigs!

When our baby wont stop crying, Mum puts a plug in it's mouth!

The nice part of me gave some toys to charity, but the rest of me was jealous!

My Mum smells lovely Just like Jam roll!

If you want wool you have to peel a sheep!

After you put Sugar in your tea you have to wind it up with a spoon!

...And Please let me lose my way to school tomorrow, but Please God, let me find my way home again!

Could I please have just one dress that I dont have to grow into?

I know why you married Dad. It was because he looks like me!

Which do I do, eat the balls, or drink the syrup?

Whats so great about being a grown up anyway that makes every body want to be one?

Mummy said that sometimes she wishes her name was anything but Mummy!

I dont know what starts off the alphabet, I havent got that far yet!

I think I must love you Mum because I Know I dont come home for the pleasure!

If theres a war, send for Jesus and the Police!

I have a special slambook just for Tantrums!

My Mum cut her hand! The doctor is taking the knitting out tomorrow!

Dont cry because the budgie died Mum. Dad will mend it when he gets home!

Mum never plays with me. She's always playing with the sink!

I can have a PUPPY because Mum said "that's all we need!"

Daddy is so lazy! He goes out all day and just watches the telly at night!

Dad, when I grow up, do I move out or do you?

After mum gives me a bath, she has to give the bath a bath!

I'm not really cheating, its just my way of winning!

Polite is when you eat the sandwiches without looking inside first!

Mum and Dad make me share everything with my sister!

I've just shared my measles!

I mustn't tell what I bought you for your birthday mum, but if you dont have any talcum powder it will come in very handy!

Invisible talking is called thinking

Shops have their lights on at night so burglars can see what theyre doing.

Im in a hurry! your goodbye kiss is on the door!

I saw a dog by a lampost trying to do ballet!

Having a baby is a very good way to slim!

Towels are for wiping the dirt off after you've washed!

I know I made you get up twice last night, and I know I made Dad get up twice too! But what about me? I was up all four times!

In the cemetery where all the dead people live, all the gravestones have phone numbers on!

If education is so important then why isn't it one of our subjects at school?

Grown up is when you wear a bra and dust up all the day!

I hate to write thankyou letters when I already got the presents!

x x x   x

My little brother gave me a big colouring book for my birthday.

It would have been nicer if he hadn't filled it in first!

Dad, I learnt something very important at school today!

The others all get more pocket-money than me!

Mum always pricks
cooking sausages
to make sure
they are dead!

Childrens faces
get dirtier than
grown ups
because they're
nearer the
ground!

Why does rain
fall in little
pieces and not
in one big lump?

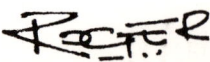